ISBN 13 : 978-1-942500-36-0
ISBN 10: 1-942500-36-0

BOULEVARD BOOKS
THE NEW FACE OF PUBLISHING

WWW.BOULEVARDBOOKS.ORG

THE ROAD LESS TRAVELLED

ERIC PIKUL

Gratuity

I'm Grateful for each and every compliment
The building blocks that stock and spark all of my confidence
The belief that grief creates a higher consciousness
Case and point greatest stories ever told were in an argument
But nowadays less people appear competent
Founding fathers on our dollars turn a mountain to a
monument
Haters smile in your face and envy every one of your
accomplishments
Frankly there's no time to waste our time so we get on with it
The good die young and the bad just remain ominous
Our president's a racist and dines on dinners with the
communists
Corrupt politicians pass information like cheap condiments
Big fish in small ponds just some visions of some dominance
Lies written by the media distorted by the columnists
Forget all of the stress but don't ever hide behind the obvious
Truth hides behind the eyes and burns alive inside the oculus
Build a bunker in your basement and prepare for the
apocalypse

Creativity

Creations in the eye hand in hand beauty's beholder
Her image touched the sun broke the mold and moved a
boulder
Creative yet so tasteless there's never any substance
Some art forms are dead based on a wrong sense of judgment
Claimed he was a cousin relations to the roots
Lies in his eyes always far from the truth
Beauty took the eye across cities and under waters
Creations of the nations first born sons and daughters
Think ahead and form facts goals guaranteed golden
Mimicked for the minute head pounding and swollen
Identity holds serenity a creators precious creeds
Living for the moment good karma in your deeds
Sacred to some Statements quoted for the press
You live to carry on improve and conquer stress
Dated if you've waited so here goes nothin else
May time master minds and define how we've felt

Apologies

Sorrys are a long shot when we mean less than more

You feel bad for what was said and pour your heart right on the floor

Apologize for mistakes made from the past throughout the present

Breathe in every scent and memorize the very essence

Let it be known before it's too late you meant every single sorry

Heart is colder than a boulder in the minds furthest quarry

Can we fathom what will happen with the difference in the distance

Wasted times a tasteless crime you better mind your minutes

Apologized ...a fathers eyes look down on his son and daughter

Harmonized a mother's mind drifts to sleep to waves of

water Parents plan for peace but not all can be foretold

Sorry doesn't cut it families fancy growing old

Bonds will carry on some forgive not all forget

Apologize before it's too late and you begin to regret

Welcome Home

Going home to where your welcomed and people value all
your stays
It's been a long road traveled countless nights turn into days
This world can be so brutal some points can leave you heartless
But no matter where you go at home is where the heart is
Welcome home to the decrepit battle torn and beaten bloody
Faces of the sacred long live the ones who've judged me
Because I'm home now all my troubles are behind
Seen and dreamed of my queen our love a whole other find
Welcome home to the lost who've found ways back to before
Whoevers on the outside is welcomed back on thru the door
Some say they can't go home and sometimes this is the truth
Things have changed in many ways the past has swallowed up
your youth
But despite either fight welcome home to all alums
Walk to beats so unique you can never find those drums
Welcome back to the facts the truth sets you free

Remember When

Remember when the beauty lived inside the eyes of the beholder

Remember when you were young and only wished you could be older

Remember the first time you did that the boss of all beginners

Remember what was ours kept it safe from all the sinners

Remember when you first met in her eyes a true connection

Always kept your guard up remember it was for protection

Remember how we tried to guess what was to come and what will happen

Remember how we never thought things thru and always acted

Remember when you reminisced and may not have liked your past

Remember you can change yourself and build a form that lasts

Remember to use your memory keep sakes and valued thoughts

Take note of past experience but let life run its course

Remember how it happened and where to change direction

Remember what you learned and take from every lesson

Remember to not forget those who've gone before us

Rememberings the message re repeat it like the chorus

Once Told...

It all started off an old promise

The demons talk tell half truths and half nonsense

Lately Been wanting the lord to

Come for me but maybe I just needed my own god to comfort
me

Soft words spoken barely uttered to be heard

Penned piece of a beast with thoughts that have burned

Where we at now negates the positive

Doing things out of hate that leaves us logic-less

The good die young I've seen the best go

And the bad are left to wait their fate on death row

Up shits creek sinking without paddles

Day by day led astray to fight hard and win battles

Good vibes coincide with nice rides and cool peoples

Dark thoughts and fought wars brings out sins and true evils

No stones unturned follow your own leader

Peter paid Paul but who paid Peter

Better

The best deserve what's better

Blessed by the words of a letter

To write for a night inspire insight for one not to fold under pressure

Trials and tributes were muttered

Words said in a breath that were stuttered

We know that we can so reach for a hand be the best out of all of the others

Strive for some pride at a price

Warm days give way to cold nights

If it's done once then make it make twice

The style filled with denial

Since the days you were just a child

You dreamt and you dreamed new views and extremes but again it's been awhile

The best can always do better

Just push and be a go getter

Marks Made...

Marks made to admire

I'll start me a fire

And burn away what's left of the past

I said I'll pick me a winner

Not a saint or a sinner

It was a dream that I wanted to last

Lord knows I was hollow

Another fling with a model

Life and time go by way too fast

But the love was for certain

Not like any other person

Shes got a style that no one gets passed

She's a lover and a fighter

Never met nobody wiser

She was a lady with a real fine craft

Maybe us two can grow old

Together travel the globe

Make memories our own personal stash

Lost Fallacies

Losing track of the fiction

Caught in voids of depiction

Some Might find joys in the wisdom

Lots of Loud noise out their system

As in all the drugs clouded their vision

They still out for one mission

Ride or Diers a couple righteous ones Wearing wires

Local boss suppliers one thought leads to off in liars

All my thoughts for hire these ideas are clear till I've retired

Waking up and I'm inspired to write what I've desired

Too much coffee now I'm wired

(Sleep is the cousin of death -DJ Effect) I'm Not tired

Balls to the wall hit the gas to get passed

Alcohol the last call last chance to get trashed

She loved the NEw York Drawl from the south and she
laughed

Get it how you live from the start till what's last

SunLight Within

New dawns ease together to start fresh days

Pay tribute to what's within you and offer all praise

The rest goes unsaid but understood just the same

This monopoly holds monotony beneath any pain

Remedies for fees a tax charged remember the total

The best bought and sought so remember who owes you

A break in the case is at stake so find an approach

Celebrate the chase and raise your glass for the toast

Halfway divided it's split down every middle

Big things will bring a bigger change to the little

Envy the simple because deep thinking won't cripple

Never undone kept tip top swept under the rug

Leftover on the shoulders so where was the love

Keep all beneath take leaps for your faith

Stay to stand not fall in your own state of grace

The Weatherman

It's those days where the skies go grey

The type of time when you find your way

I'm talking trips that'll take you there

The kind of look that'll meet your stare

Signify what's said before long

And hum the tune of your personal war song

Half given values seen are more than were held

Play the game you were given and the cards you were dealt

Written words mix letters spell messages for the masses

Taught lessons thru my blessings you can't learn in your

classes The path less gone is the road I travel

The war was won by beasts in battle

Trained for trains buses commutes to compute

On the way to get paid each day then reboot

Styles all your own learned and picked for pursuit

Pick apart all the hearts and your a great in your group

End of Questions

Death to decisions hide behind complexities

Obedient to ingredients called on by the recipes

Fall flat without stats as a whole or collectively

Drawn conclusions patterns in the mix of what matters

Built from the ground up climb high up the ladders

3 strikes in the fight go and swing with the batters

Aim for another era time ticks for that triumph

Seconds stand for a plan heart beats of a lion

Alone to yourself no one else on your island

Nothing set in stone the granites grand with the grandeur

Songs sing and grow wings time to follow the cantor

Back and forth is a chore but someone has to banter

Forthcoming for fairness let's commit to what's right

Beaten bloody and bruised but stood through the fight

Rise high as the sky and use all your might

The dark plays its part but everyday gives its light

Whole

Farewell to forevers hidden meanings in a rush

Painting pictures in the scriptures write the wrongs with
your brush

Set aside all your pride find what's mentioned through the
touch

Relics relished in the old beneath all the dust

Hands held to unite grip the greats when you trust

Love lingers in the fingers paced and placed when it's lust

Significant and Different the guides give their guidance

Defeated never beaten defy the odds through defiance

Count on contacts for the rest be assured through reliance

Gone for gold now your old stories told of king Midas

A miracle so spiritual not explained by a science

Made in the shade partners persist through alliance

Maybe all those other halves can come and make you

whole You dig so big the days you live and bury every hole

What isn't yours to keep when they sleep then you stole

Learn from being burned till the day you grow old

WWWWWH

Heed the warnings of the calling

Answers soaring skies are falling

Where the sky meets the suns rays

Where the lord goes on Sundays

Picture perfect isn't worth it

But not to try is always worthless

Most will purchase without purpose

Some will worship this life's circus

When times call to come pray

When the prices have been raised

Paid for pity lonely cities

Dollar bills and punch drunk diddys

What comes up after long days

What's been done in the wrong ways

It's been said that talk is cheap

The kind of kind that's been called weak

Who needs what they can keep

Who dreams of a plan b

A Letter...

Dear today goodbye tomorrow

We're in the now on time that's borrowed

This moment we own it now that's a fact

Regrets cause stress no going back

The presents a present so value events

Even if it's a snippet or a time to vent

Appreciate being late or always on time

Either way seize the day the seconds will shine

You get what u give no need to remind

Embrace your fate the faith is a find

Tired yet inspired as the minutes diminish

Hyped for the night as the days come to finish

What's to come may have already been done

History repeats but not all has begun

Time is priceless no time to price it

The future will bring ends and a mends to crisis

Fathers Days

Eloquence the element saturated through the titles Fellowship

so relevant we've made it many miles

Harden with the hardships give way to the grief

The good die young and not all practice what they preach I'll

miss you and you'll miss me and one day we'll meet again A

father made me smarter my pops was also my best friend

Some years back he taught me that and also showed me this A

father's son true indeed Rest In Peace you will be missed

Cemetery stones are cold the facts are always colder

My memories have given me ways to see you as I grow older

A son never forgets those days yankee games and never
hungry

This man always provided mom and I were always lucky An

angel who fights my demons god bless you and your halo Dad

was superman to me the man could never say no Happy

Fathers Days Dad a son never forgets

You'll always be remembered pops I swear on your last breath

Rejoice

Give a voice to the smiles and the happiness within

For life is joyful now tell some strangers and your kin

Smiles are contagious bring on moods the masses miss

Vintage venues on the menu time tells tales that reminisce

Believe you me rejoice where there's a will always a way

Not all skies are bright but sun shine will seize the day

Positive and promised pick and choose the next advance

Smile and believe pick your tools to build your chance

Starting from the bottom rising up to be a Phoenix

The rise seen thru eyes of all those who've ever seen it

Demons can be conquered the good fight is won in battle

Overturn and overcome adversaries in your shadow

Freedom comes when joy takes you to the top

You appreciate the rise when you yourself has dropped

There's no difference in commitment you'll find yourself in time

Rejoice upon the hour leave the negatives behind

The Storms Way

Always caught in a storm

Rains more when it pours

You were bought when you were born

Open doors are the laws

And you fought for your form

Chosen wars for the cause

Just for sport you keep warm

Wrote a force for applause

Just a thought till it's gone

Get the source on the horn

Just a sight filled with scorn

And no sweat goes to waste

Worked hard just to taste

Don't let the cards seal your fate

You've come too far just to wait

Faceless

Neither friend nor an enemy

Faceless with no real identity

Transparent yet generic thoughts grandiose

You've heard a lot about it now you see for yourself

A reputation proceeds its own seat on the thrown

A desire to own a bit of the unknown

They retired and rehired the cycle repeats

Pens to pads and on papers written in peace

The rhythms unique songs where the sinners will preach

Faceless and so tasteless a combination of grief

Better from the fed up then its hit and release

Letters never let up the beast will be brief

The pressure is forever and the weak will

delete

The weather couldn't be better one wish is a beach

Now get up and go get em cause this city won't sleep

Pain

All Pain is precious

That's whats said in its daily message

A Waste of time if it's not accepted

You succumb and there's no exception

You feel numb when you lose direction

Pain can push gives a new connection

Write your wrongs with a true correction

Pain is strong hear a true confession Makes you stronger it's
the newest blessing

Call up karma told her drop her weapon

Too much armor there's no honor in that PROtection

So much calmer after trauma give me 4 Seconds

No shame in pain and that's without questions

A stain so strained from all the infections

Brings change to brains through each of the lessons

Against the grain it's the pain that gives conscious conceptions

Sacrificed Freedoms

Freedom is withheld sacrificed for something stable

Dig into your desire to do what's always saved you

Don't fight what comes natural you need to feed your passions

To like your life forget the hype as all the rest happens

We're all here and fear what's to come from our actions

Don't stress what's next accept the minor moments and reactions

Do what makes you feel good give into what you've wanted

Inner voices making noises listen up they're always honest

Others give opinions be wary what they promise

Tears can shape careers blood and sweat can make the content

Milestones on your own just listen to your conscience

Follow what your heart says don't pay mind to all the nonsense

Appreciate

These letters form words that told the past as in a pretense

Ran to plan for bigger breaks and swore to pledge allegiance

No complaints no negativity we store no types of grievance

Hard work beats the talented and all of their achievements

We blink and think just one life lived it flashes passed but faster

They told us all to go to school but what do we do after

Don't live to work just work to live invest your best in laughter

They said your life's an open book I'm stuck on the first chapter

Born to carry on a name from my father it was given

His memory lives on today he'd talk and I would listen

Actions speak the loudest became my fathers mission

Taught me how to be a man instilled the realest wisdom

My dearest mother, strongest woman ,always I'd admire

Forever appreciated your support doesn't expire

A mothers instinct never fails or starts to even tire

Thanks for showing me the way ma forever you inspire

The Last Stand

Battle till you're an adult but the fights always continue

To eats always a treat despite a lack of choices on the menu

Nervous without a purpose out of sight and out of mind

You fight the good fight daily everyday you find the time

Way up in age you pick to choose just how the fight will last

You think about the days regrets and leave them in the past

When we can find the time we exercise our mind

Intent was just to shine and make what's left all mine

It's time to take possession responsible for what we've done

They say we crawl to walk and eventually we'll run

Take up arms as if your last stands right around the next turns corner

What you need is true indeed so think what completes your order

Drowning down without the crown can't breathe with all this water

Lost in what's beneath your feet it's shits creek that leads to slaughter

Last stands have just been taken never decide to give right up

They say that it's a legends myth but always trust in touch

Some say it's Mind over matter

But Never think your mind doesn't matter

Work hard to climb up the ladder

To live to work makes this life so much sadder

Read in between lines and Remember every chapter

Brighten up your life know each feeling that'll capture

Think about what's next when your put

out to pasture

Practice what you preach to his flock said the pastor

The fake cannot relate real recognize an actor

Gone before the guilt eternally a life after

Goodbye to the lies and the life of a bachelor

Feel it hard in the heart someone else's feelings matter

The Sun Shines and Gives the Light

Lives in the day and dies at night

But never sets with out a fight

Wakes you up strong and bright

Grows the trees to bigger heights

A daily Symbol of our life

Makes the wine and all the rice

Feeds the fauna proves the price

The sun can shine and ease the mind

Brightens paths the rest you find

It grows the grass and measures time

The sun is yours the sun is mine

Speechless

Where have all the words gone when there's nothing left to say

We talk our way out and other times to stay

Speak when spoken to is the mantra of our day

But Where have all the words gone when there's nothing left to say

Sometimes we talk to hear ourselves other times to shine and speak

They say actions are louder and all the talk is cheap

Words are weapons on their own accord and at times can be deep

So say what you really mean don't just talk while your asleep

Words speak thru pens to paper and voice volumes about the writer

Some things are best left unsaid to resonate and to inspire

Quotes not always timeless but burn the mind like fire

Remember what I've said before I've gone off and retired

The words will carry on every letters a survivor

There are no words sometimes but every breath can make you tired

Pictures paint a thousand words the truth sets free a liar

People say what they please which means all speak how they desire

Be True

A vision and mission that lead you to listen

The lies will breed a lack of new wisdom

A challenge to chance the truth will enhance

Dishonesty is obviously the devils

Dance

To thine own self keep true quoted and noted

A promise to my conscience the lies just withhold it

The truth can set free all those in prison

By the shame of the pain and the lies of the system

Vicious cycles are an eyeful fight fire with fire

Beat deceit when you defeat and make a liar retire

March to drums all your own

When we can't go home

And keep honest that's a promise

Because Before a liars storm its always the calmest

True stories are best told and cherished forever

Signed and sealed always real that's the end of this letter

Creation's Lesson

Mother Earth and Father Time

Hand in hand they make life shine

Moving forward can't rewind

Can't look back the world is mine

We move ahead improved indeed

Learned from the past how to succeed

All bets are off we've filled our need

But life goes on the more we breathe

Ships are jumped in search of new

Avoid the lies and seek what's true

So Get the most forget the few

But don't move on without a clue

Gone for now but not forgotten

Live to give the more you'll blossom

Think it thru you'll find an option

And Overcome any problem

The Maverick

Above average and half savage

It's the maverick that casts magic

Lives lavish with bad habits

Saw tragic but had to have it

Can't grasp it but can manage

No status but don't panic

Low taxes and low attics

Gold batches and cold sabbaths

An old mattress some dope addicts

The flows spastic there's no access

Cold plastic and no damage

A grown actress some lit matches

The tones passive but's been active

Shopped at saks fifth and went batshit

The whole package the growths massive it's the maverick that flows acid

Maze of My Mind

My mind is a maze a path of conception

Where seeing is believing in every direction

Ideas and some fears followed by a question

Take a right at insight hang left at each lesson

Pass by all the why's stop by each suggestion

There's Danger by the anger don't get close to aggression

Keep your eyes on the pride many forms of expression

Speed past any wrath past an idea's inception

Drive fast pass the past memories of the conscience

Opinions in a prison barred down by the content

Pit stops at the tops of day dreams and the nonsense

Think big start to dig deep thru the sub conscious

Lost when the minds clear need to steer with a compass

Dreams made of scenes with no kinds of hardship

Nightmares cause a scare then you wake up to reality

My mind is a maze that'll bring the best out of me

Tired of Technology

No more phones I pads or even a tablet

Before we're broken the world needs a break from their
gadgets

Service not at your service you fly into a panic

Social media has our social skills in a state so tragic

We love all our likes and the easier access

But youngsters lost their hunger just to even be active

Digital criminals thieve IDs and wreak lots of havoc

Pics get hits crush self esteems of the average with no plastic

Before apps and attachments there was actual action

People shared how they cared and you saw their reaction

Now people hide behind screens too preoccupied to even

dream As long as there's streams and we can send out some

memes Eyes blank stare out Downwind with no hunger

If google is your usual whose the cousin of slumber?

How did we get by as hunters out in the tundra?

We're always asking why and can't explain why we wonder

Beauty and it's Beholder

Beauty started in the eye of the composer

The soldier of love fell in love when he locked eyes with
the beholder

The storm before the calm there's the right and there's the
wrong that's what they told her

Parameters for amateurs and seeing is believing

Morning is for mourning and breathings for the evening

Atest to a test the best leave marks before leaving

Beauty's what they saw you left it at the door how do they
see you?

A view that's caused anew something simple something true

The beauty's within you its been seen thru and thru

The beholders getting colder but the eyes will never lie

Beauty's all around us if you ever wonder why

This world can be ugly....

LimBo

No gravity in my world so we just float thru life

Up in the air without a care it could be day or night

Write the wrongs with better values until it's part of life

But sometimes you'll find limbo a place to roll the dice

When things just aren't settled and there's nothing set in stone

You try to make your stake to create a better home

So add your tries and triumph and life will throw a bone

Others walk in your shoes you're not in this alone

Calmed down just to coast in limbo like some ghosts

Set sail without fail on boats built for growth

Get going on your vote and say it with your throat

This world is cold with out a coat but we never give up hope

Lady Luck

You risk it all with Lady Luck

To lose it all or make a buck

She plays her games and takes her cut

She'll place your bets and play for keeps

The price is high your chance is cheap

This life's alive these things get deep

Respect the lady wish her well

Her will is strong she casts her spell

She gives to take and lives to tell

Carries on throughout all ages

Wrote the book on old ripped pages

The good the bad and all the phases

Cold as stone she can be vicious

Some lose some win she causes sickness

She takes her tolls she wants your riches

She's here nor there it's only business

Watch out for

Lady Luck

Better YET

How can I push on and improve

Day to day to enlighten my views

Better yet wash away the old news

Move ahead to a point your enthused

Better yet time to win and not lose

Speed ahead to the point you will choose

Better yet forge ahead and pay dues

Set the pick and pick up on the clues

Better yet move on and make strides

Own your offense and let it change tides

Better yet be the one on the rise

Everyone knows by the look in your eyes

Better yet see thru all go and thrive

The competition was brought down to size

Better yet learn the lessons be wise Stay

focused with your eye on the prize

BETTER YET... THE BEST IS YET TO COME

Reality Never Betrayed Me

Testify to fantasize and leave actuality

Broke apart an open start relied on reality

Betrayal by the false the fake is filled with fault

The real has got a feel that never leaves the vault

Cherish those hysterics what's made up has no leverage

More than just a message we drink to think beyond the beverage

Reprieved past our need to see the truth retrieved

Reliably reliable reality is viable to what too many tried to do

Like they fired and rehired you

The truth Won't be concealed

It's about a bigger deal that will always be revealed

But has it ever done me wrong

Never has... we respect the form

Writing lyrics with some spirits who sang on some old song

And So the tune goes on

Thru and thru Learned something new everyday since I was born

Shades of Grey

Opposites like two poles cold like those places

They say there's shades of grey black and white are so
tasteless

That's an understatement in the placement of greatness

The little things in life take the cake for being sacred

Intricate legitimate in all forms of nature

Value every detail that was given by your maker

Regrets are nothing less then realizing what's right later

Seeing every angle makes the alpha not the beta

We need to see so evenly how things are created

Remember every piece so the image isn't faded

They say we can't be judged but forever we'll be rated

Shades of grey create each day without them each is naked

Honest in intent so the truth will be exposed

Lies live on in eyes even if the truth was sold

Forget the black and white shades of grey

Make the gold

Remember what's been said don't just do as your told

OutSpoken

No longer stifled Mr Pikul

Of course the thoughts delightful

Speech free as it's spoken

The mind is an ocean

Open to ideas

The thoughts not always clear

And as they come near

We say what might appear

Imagine saying words without a consequence

No one judges your intent

But they rise to your defense

America the great home of the heavyweights

A one of a kind place where our freedom is at stake

So here's a resolution to compliment our constitution

Maybe a solution to said outspoken type pollution

Say what you achieve or what your heart perceives

This is why we breathe for freedom to be believed

Carry On

Carry on throughout the towns the daily ups the daily downs

Carry on beyond your grounds take in the sights and all the sounds

Carry on just like tradition open your eyes to deeper visions

Carry on for better systems learn this life thru instilled wisdoms

Carry on just to carry which creates strengths in peaks and valleys

Carry on for the family have your own when your married

Carry on for the earth the air we breathe the ground and dirt

Carry on for the hurt the pain will push and prove its worth

Carry on despite what's happened you talk the talk but lack the action

Carry on for all your passions hard work can hurt but betters rations

Carry on just because fight good fights to win your wars

Carry on to an applause better vibes will open doors

Carry on for what's to come you just can't help what has been done

Carry on when on the run a busy body knows a ton

Carry on or you'll be carried the truth can hurt but makes you savvy

Carry on and you'll be happy carry on and do exactly.... What you need

Ever long

A love that never dies and after life immortalized

No matter how many tries we never gave up our love survived

It braved the test of time and needed no life line

A love that's justified harmonized each other's eyes

It goes on never ending what we have there's no pretending A

heart beats on the same song we carry on forever long Darkest

before the dawn she's my light that lifts each storm Together

we carry on never torn between false forms

No one knows me like you do puppy love that stood and grew

We lift ourselves up when we're stuck our love forever more
than lust

Never broke a bond of trust when I shine you shine we'll never
rust

Who would've thought Yesterday's crush would lead to a life
long kind of rush

The first time I made her blush she was addicted to my touch

And until death do us part ever long she'll have my heart

Uncertain

Uncertain type of person but really whose for sure

Up in the air without the sights set on any type of cure

We always want the pure something that we've known before

But we don't know what's in store and what we all need to endure

Uncertain unassuming when and where do we start blooming

For those with no wins sick of losing

We can turn the burnt right back to booming

We control this movement let's start moving

Uncertainty is adversity masked within disguise

The unknown can grab the thrown if we don't hold on as advised

Sick of all the shock but we will come out on top

Just conceive that you believe in your own dreams to beat the clock

If time is of the essence every minute is a present

We learn new lessons in the seconds that tick on to give suggestions

So forget the stress from fear of what's to come

What happens next you will accept don't run from what's not
done

The Night OF

A poets prose pushed for passage

I own my soul thoughts so Socratic

A story of glory gives only more guts

A teachers testimony put forth to touch

The grit goes to govern the greats and those gone

We live for ourselves spirits carry on

We delve to dabble in different distinctions

And enlist to exist to move past extinction

No glory without guts the story agrees

Life leaves a free lunch few and far between

Learn from the past resist repetition

Ignorance insists we submit no revision

Change from the same against the grain on your mission

Most talk is too cheap just shut up and listen

No price put on passage or the right of

Celebrate the great day in town the night of

The End

Spent and sent here in due time

Gets so tense it can chill spines

It's been awhile but it's final for all

Call your friends it's the end of the Ending

The real deal there's no time for pretending

You fought for sport and always gave it your all

So many roads lead to goals for the bold

So many holes dug too deep for the gold

The end is near crystal clear like you've seen it all

All good things have to come to a close

Like the crack in concrete that gave growth to the rose

Without sky showers suns devour and put an end to it all

When it rains it pours and less is more

From coast to shore we end the war

At the least Bring peace from the east onto all

We fall then we get up till the end we won't let up and of
course that's the coarse for us all....

Ode To Ends

We knew each other's deepest truths

So I know you when it isn't you

The love can only go so far when different views

Have us doubting news and counting moves

Those arguments you love to win but hate to lose

Now it's time for us to pick and choose

We tried and tried but lost the vibe

You think I'm bad then try and find a different guy

And what you need I can't conceive

I guess we've grown apart so let me breathe

Cause when you wake up alone you'll think of me

I gAve it my best shot and only got extra grief

We can keep it short we need to grieve

There's no other way to say I need to leave... I need to leave

Influential...

The wind flows on and behooves you to move

Sunshine warms your mind and improves any mood

The weather relieves pressure as soon as the storms pass

Nature feeds the leaves and in time grows tall grass

Leaves fall to the floor in the fall call it autumn

All the Trees change to yellow brown red and some orange

In between fall and spring winter freezes the scene

Wind Chills keep it still as we dream for some green

So the birds say their words wait for spring till they sing

The ants and the plants seasons brings living things

Always wonder when summer wakes Mother Earth from her slumber

Heat hits those high numbers like no others

So we're Speechless on the beaches sand inside both my sneakers

In the water for a quarter as sea creatures come to greet us

The seasons are the reasons were inside or on the outs

Influential a crescendo to stay or get up off the couch

StaBLe

Get involved in the joy and deploy some stability

The best is left unsaid move ahead with ability

The calm before the storm can better form and virility

Never stumble stick to humble be a pro in humility

Practice what you preach pass it on thru fertility

When you got it figured out and your able to be stable

There's food on the table and this world placed a label

People surround your cradle tend to be the ones who shape

you

Smooth sailing for the captain who drove the boat with
passion

If you can make it happen see it thru with every action

Keep calm in the caption because you'll always be a

fraction

A piece of the best we invest in what's next

Never settle for what's less it's more stress on ur chest

Pay all your debts no regrets to digest

Fine for the future be the winner of the losers

No defeat can be measured with a ruler

Live for the moment because beggars can't be choosers

You Yourself and Your

Came from a cold and bold component

Whoever you are you best own it

Alone in my zone my own opponent

Me against myself I don't condone it

Fight the good fight to win most battles

Celebrate as a great escape to the shadows

Headed in right directions minus the arrows

Deep beneath thoughts most answers in the shallows

This world helps shape and create your identity

The vibes always live walk near feel my energy

A foe of a foe is always a friend to me

Can be kind but not weak ask any enemy

So you might just expect the best kind of intention

Create something new receive different attention

Find peace through release we let go of all tension

Forgive don't forget the rest need not be mentioned

Time

"I thought about it in the past but make it happen now because
tomorrow is the future "

Say good bye to yesterday open windows to tomorrow

Embrace a new taste and drift away from the sorrow

Because there's no point like the present for a change

The same is insane so begin to rearrange

We all have our doubts till the money's in the mouth

When you need to figure out time will tell what you're about

Father Time sees no crime in seizing every moment

Never misuse minutes seize seconds and own it

The stop watch never stops no rewinds of sun shine

The days carry on gets dark here comes time

The hour glass doesn't last sand falls back into the past

Open wounds healed by noon ocean moons go down soon

From newborns and new toons to old ruins and old tombs

The thought of time will consume the best will shine over
doom

Status Quo

Sentiments are generous status is the question

Left without a team of doubt perseverance is the lesson

When things are just ok and you get on thru the day

We want our feelings high as ceilings but we're learning our own way

Crows and Ravens are in tow sentiments of Edgar Poe

Sometimes our spirits grow over cups of Joe and Co

But then our Lowest of the lows look for that status quo

Karmas a black mamba whose bite always knows

Who and what deserves when actions speak they're always heard

When life ever throws its curves therapy is reached through words

Poetic in each message the speech beyond excessive

There always is an exit if we stay the course and be progressive

So the status is selective and we all must be aggressive

The go getters are the winners cold souls who wait will freeze like winters

Both Saints and sinners show up for dinners

To feed is just a need but some who succeed are overfilled
with greed

We all must believe in more to plant the seed so we rise to the
occasion and build to achieve

Waves of Wrath

Hell hath no fury like a storm at sea

He who braves the waves earns a new degree

O captain of fortune you win to claim defeat

As your ship insists these waves of wrath you clear the path to meet

Gods green earth has so much blue respect the waters hold

For generations across nations these stories have been told

Respect is earned not given out the seas rage will scream and shout

So many go and leave without and even more will dream about

Decisions so decisive white caps will sit on top

Nothing colder than the sea when the sun begins to drop

The night is dark and drowns the water in never ending darkness

People set a sail without fail to throw away their garbage

Forget the forgotten move on and some would say they're heartless

The ocean can keep a secret like there was no other

Only speak when spoken with your words have drowned when muttered

....Repercussions....

Penalties are generally definitions you deserve

Easier said than done when you have a way with words

Actions can speak louder golden silence gives you power

The stench of desperation won't wash off within the shower

Time to reflect to figure out what's next

We think we all know best until it's time to test

They say more is less in any given quest

Walk a mile in their shoes to view a mans steps

Stand tall and strong it's darkest before the dawn

You always pay to play so choose the right over the wrong

Time to change the tune and sing a different song

Wave goodbye to the ride and dream on thru the yawns

Always over under flip the script to change the tale

If you never try to change you accepted that you failed

These words are more provisions rations for your rationale

Move on from the wrong and reason will prevail

Broken

To fix what's in hand makes you more of a man

Till Broke do we boast give coats to the ghosts

Warm up the past so our futures will last

If broken we fix it the unknown dismiss it

In love with our flaws it adds to our cause

So stand and applaud give thanks to your lord

The Broken's devotion stays open to motion

And making the moves enhances your moods

So let's go and get it can't wait for the credits

Broken to pieces we pick up in sequence

The teachers will teach us but some just won't reach

us All souls in the hole don't make to a mold

The Broken need fixin and that's done thru wisdom

See scenes with your vision hear clear when you listen

Makes sense to the system the broken have risen

Adapt to the facts and what breaks we put back .... Together

...Nothing Less...

Nothing less than success to a dream

Played the best but what's next for the rest of the team

Not selfish but selfless ...can't help those who've become cold
and helpless

So I've gone for the gusto that's it in a nutshell...

Everyday is a struggle when the rain pours in puddles

Go to work for the muscle we live and breathe hustle

Nothing less or maybe more...so we're fighting all these battles
just to win another war

Nothing less so forget this stress it's a

Mess that'll tend to cheat to possess

Count what's blessed when we know what's best after you've
carried on and seen what's next

We move on after we've had some rest so bare your crest live
that life and pass that test because we can't accept.... Nothing
Less....

Better Half

Strive to be alive from your 9 to your 5

The better side that makes you do a lot more than survive

Change with tides and turn blind eyes to looks that tell lies

The kind of vibe that says if you fall then you too will rise

The half that will last for years after your past

Half the glass is full before and after your task

Laugh as they pass a chance to dance this life is too fast

Dangerous it's made for us no way can they label us

Some say it's just the way we lust maybe we're notorious

My better part that gave me heart always knew right from the start

We set apart to make the art bright at night to light the dark

No knowledge just some things we know

Together we make life beautiful

Can't breathe without so hear me out

No need to fear or scream and shout

My half is best others can't be considered

Cold as they come well be gone till the winter

TALK is CHEAP...

Humble as they mumble

The talks cost is spoken

Wisdom comes in bundles

Words are drowned in the ocean

Stand tall to never stumble

Movements made without motion

Torn to never tumble

Debt is owed to devotion

Expressed in excess without exits

How can we leap to leave ?

Made one too many messes

And still we breathe to breed

Can't take steps without stresses

Speak the speech that's built for speed

Too many No's will lead to Yes's

Talk is cheap a beach of greed

MOTIVATION

I've been down and back up from the peaks to those valleys

Learned to fall and get up through the streets and those alleys

The broken and torn the lives of the scorned are my
motivation

Stressed from success or a lack of progress never regress carry
on and be motivated

Reach deep within ignore the war on your sins squint and see
how to win envision your motivation

They say to fall hard is half but to get up and laugh put failed
attempts in the past just might motivate

You as in You your-self as in who these effects will affect to
push on and infect others with motivation

The lowest of lows where the chance and the hopes glow till
they grow high as the sky it all starts from a look in the eye of
those motivated

So fall down but get up and live with some trust enough is
enough what is your motivation?

Break Aw@y

Break away from normality

Lie awake and dream far away from reality

A new place without a taste for the fallacy

Break away from the days just for salary

Lay away and payments made are an allergy

Every man is a Mickey in search of his Mallory

Break away from grey days in the gallery

Lose the blues and shed the weight like a calorie

Break away from today sit and pray with a Valkyrie

Touch the sky and justify heavens right above your balcony

Teach the old anew and pave the ways with your alchemy

Break away but never fade to the shade of your hourly

Stay in a state of grace keep the pace with your Calvary

Live with no regrets passed all tests that empower me

So make that change to the same wash away the stains of the pain and just....break away...

EAGER Egos

Coming from the common peoples

Living long to fight the evils

Wrote the song before the sequels

Painting pics without the easels

American as all bald Eagles

Stood up to all pins and needles

RIP John carry on just like the Beatles

Caught all the flicks by Tarentino

Broke the curse of big bambinos

Spent the rent in a clubs casino

Smokin ciggs and countin seagulls

Bigger heads and eager egos

While they and them call us equals

Foolish fools and stormy steeples

Drank the drink to taste the vino

Subjects of Sunsets in el caminos

Guiding LiGHt

Illuminating all within the light

Breaks thru the dark and ends the night

It guides me....

Let's me see and view we've grown anew

We've walked and talked tried through and through   It guides me....

The grasp won't last what's shaped the past is gone for now far
from the town

It changed me....

What's next is left to wait for fate defiance to be true in haste

It's calling....

.

So bright not a shadow cast a broken hand that shakes too fast

The light shines....

It shows a path a chance for change it lights the sky and braves the rain

It's steady....

My guiding light just let me see how I should live so the world agrees

It guides me....

Far gone for some but never lost it sheds its light as food for thought

My guiding light....

Divided We Fall

So they stand with a plan to divide by colors
I'll be damned if their klan can deny my brothers
Race religion not partitions a country built on immigration
We all came one in the same used differences to build a
nation
Ignorance can't limit this we've come too far to get regressive
All must unite to fight this plight and continue on toward true
progression
The government holds covenants and sympathizes with the
hatred
Donald Trump is just a punk as our president we'll never
make it
A radical attitude will beat and break down our nations spirit
Certainly diversity combats their wrath because they fear it
We the people see the evils and won't stand for that division
Carry on and end these wrongs has to be our only mission
Neo nazis cannot stop me these confederates are derelicts
You hate Blacks, Browns, and the North but without us you
won't exist
I pledge allegiance to deeper meanings unity to reign supreme
This is the land of the free and we all will continue to live our
dream

Free ESCAPE

There's much more than free escapes

Sounds of towns wait to alleviate

No need to chase bait to abbreviate

At any rate, a fakes face is a piece of cake

When recognized the lies lay as plain as day to eyes

Which rectifies these tests of time not SSIs but deeper
meanings only to be discovered when under the covers
dreaming

These false phonies are easily forgotten the real cronies can
seize their seeds of options and plant solutions to problems

And out grow opportunity for unity against those divided ; On
the fence hence the past tense... You were invited

Still undecided you used to be excited but now cringe and
binge on what's left within what half full glass mines filled to
the brim

LoVE is Defined

Spoken words always uttered barely heard above the kiss

A promise through a sonnet to live in love is to exist

A second chance at life breathe a breath of air that's new

His heart was picked apart and came back together when he saw you

Words of beauty can't do justice I'll stop time to have more for us

This relationship set sail to tell a tale that's more than lust

There's Romeos there's Juliets but only one you and one me

Can't replace a face that holds your place steals the stars and drinks the sea

Girl when I was young my mother spoke and said that it'd be clear

I dreamt about the day we met awoke and shed a tear

Not from the stress of sadness a river flowed from happiness

And from the day we met I lived on without regret

May we cherish what's been given this perfection may come close

Celebrate our faith in fate let's raise our glasses for a toast

PAinted WORDs

Used to listen with a vision pictures painted in the words

Now we've Risen with some wisdom put some action in our verbs

Generations change the nations but who really made the difference

Plugged into the computers may the message move the distance

Change is of the essence Q for quintessential

Smoke and drink while we think how our body is our temple

Take it back to dreams on loose leaf written down in pencil

Fast track to current stats I need my vision and my dental

401 Ks the only way or maybe more sick days

These interviews I'll list a few can change the way I'm paid

Funny how we live for our livings were defined by our trade

Then we work till it hurts and take our seats in the shade

And so we live on in our families the memory will never fade

Of course history repeats itself it stays on every page

FAMILY Jeans

Inherited dads anger and moms complexity

So I question what's been destined from directions of my
recipe

Asking all the angels decisions done with demons

There's got to be psychology behind why were breathin

Talk throuh that surface level the words are just for show

Can't talk about the top without coming from below

Appreciate completed states accomplish what's been

planned Been behind in different times that turns a boy into

a man A writer and a fighter the pen swings like the sword

An economy of harmony so let's strike a chord

Time is precious is the message can't rewind behind the
moment

Regrets can cause stress so live this life with a focus

Reluctance in abundance can put a stop

to future fortunes

Nothing ever guaranteed except more taxes and our coffins

So live like today's your one your only your chance for something true

Forget what misdirects carry on and just be you

TRY for Triumph

Hey Eric you done fucked up

But People make mistakes and that's just tough luck

It gets to the point where enough is enough

Some claim to change games but they never know rough

So to walk in some shoes of some dude with the blues

Rebels without a cause or celebs on the news

Maybe a crazy lady whose just hooked on her booze

Or a man with a plan but he just can't choose

The options will stop him the man or the martian

Our Minds are concoctions not used become rotten

So we get high off toxins to end all our problems

And the fear of us stoppins in our ears like some Johnson and Johnson

We'll prevail in our Gotham well strive and well blossom

Taylor made in the shade can't give up like adoption

A tribute to triumph hearts pump blood of a lion

And thru the storms of Poseidon well keep on defyin.... ALL
ODDS

Friends ARE Family

Met as youngsters teens on a team

Only child in the wild trying to figure out a dream

No brothers or sisters family could be closer

But my friends made that mends cool to crash on the sofa

Brothers not by blood but it's always been by love

Some fell victim to the system none of us would ever judge

Color never mattered we always only saw our family

Drunk passed the test who else would drive my Camry

The years added on best friends for double digits

Now it's whose having kids and wifeys washing dishes

Change is good knock on wood but we'll never burn our
bridges

Real recognize real most other dudes act like bitches

I put this on my crew just the ones who've seen me through

Last calls for alcohols bar brawls and BBQs

No homo but the love is timeless here's to talking shit till
we're old and blinded

MY FRIENDS ARE FAMILY

Cupids CHOKEHOLD

Hearts burn with desire the love won't retire

One more chance at least just a dance

How you move might inspire if you sell I'm your buyer

At First glance you can call it romance

Real love is a drug a buzz sent from above

Make the plans for the trips and the tans

Not built to judge just melt that grudge with a hug

Drop a grand on the meal and the band

Announce what amounts will you be my spouse

I propose maybe Cupids choke holds

We're in this together I knew the day that I met her

There'd be a time she'd be hooked on my line

Without further Adu I give me on to you

Forget the past let's grasp hold of the moment

No rush but it's us let's put in all our trust cause it's ours and
we know that we own it

www.ingramcontent.com/pod-product-compliance
Lightning Source LLC
Chambersburg PA
CBHW072208090426
42740CB00012B/2433